22 ways to say *black*

CREATIVE DIRECTOR Stephen Todd
ARTISTIC DIRECTION Hector Castro & Josh Hight
EDITOR Alexandra Marshall
CONTRIBUTING WRITERS Ashley Baker & Elizabeth Shapouri
FASHION ASSISTANT Gretchen Owen
PROJECT MANAGER Nathalie Rauscher
PRODUCTION AND DISTRIBUTION Éditions Dilecta, 4 rue de Capri, 75012 Paris, France
PRINTER Grafiche Marini Villorba, Via Nobel 4, 31020 Villorba (Treviso), Italy

COVER Dress - Martin Grant, Photography - Scheltens & Abbenes

PHILLIPS DE PURY & COMPANY
Thierry Nataf - Senior Vice President, Alexander Gilkes - Business Development Director
SWAROVSKI ELEMENTS
Markus Lampe - Senior Vice President Marketing, Stephen Todd - Director Branding & Communication
Lila Thibault - Senior Segment Manager, Nathalie Rauscher - Communication Manager

Published by Swarovski AG, Droeschistrasse 15, 9495 Triesen, Principality of Liechtenstein

ISBN: 978-3-033-02373-4

CONTENTS

For auction date,
viewing hours, and estimates,
visit **www.swarovski-elements.com/black**

Preface

One year ago, Swarovski asked 22 of fashion's leading designers and most promising rising talents to create one very special black dress each incorporating SWAROVSKI ELEMENTS, the standard-bearer of precision-cut crystal since 1895. A black dress because, throughout the modern era, it is the one item a woman's wardrobe is considered deficient without. The "little black dress," as it has come to be called, has become one of fashion's great ideals and the designers who created the dresses in this book have each, in their own way, explored its possibilities of form, function, mood, and adornment. Whether by Giorgio Armani, Vivienne Westwood, Alexis Mabille, Thakoon, Lanvin's Alber Elbaz, or Jean Paul Gaultier, each of these dresses represents a singular vision of a fashion archetype, executed by a master of their craft.

Now, along with Phillips de Pury & Company, the leading auction house for contemporary art and culture, Swarovski is offering these unique pieces up in a way they can do the most good. In September 2010, at Phillips' New York gallery, at 450 West 15th Street, all 22 dresses will be sold at auction to benefit the American Cancer Society and la Ligue nationale contre le cancer in France. One hundred percent of the proceeds will go to the two charities, as well as all profits from the sale of this book.

And so we present 22 Ways to Say Black.

Alexandra Marshall

*M*OURNING *has* broken: becoming "*The* new B*LACK*"

Hats off to a masterful feat: the "little black dress." Though Gabrielle Chanel did not invent it, in 1926, she most definitely put it on the map. "The Ford," it was dubbed by the journalists of *Vogue* magazine's American edition, who predicted a resounding success to parallel that of the car produced by the American industrialist. This was, after all, the beginning of the era of equality.

And so the little dress, a simple black crepe sheath with long fitted sleeves, would become the uniform of the modern woman. Restrained, disconcertingly simple, the dress cut straight to the essentials, based on a fluid line that both concealed and revealed its secret. This was certainly due to the absolute black, a shade that, in scientific terms, is not even really a color.

Black encompasses an entire story: complex, captivating, and even passionate, with multiple contradictions swirling around it. From the dawn of time, black has acted as both the agent of redemptive good and the standard of diabolical evil. Merely conjure up the term "black mass," and the duality of these two terms immediately becomes clear in a ceremony that apes liturgy, but with a very different purpose.

9

Black has long been associated with darkness and, by extension, with death and with nothingness—hence its use as a color representing mourning. Yet black is also considered the pinnacle of respectability: as opposed to a garish red or a luminescent blue, it is in no way ostentatious. By the Middle Ages, it would become the very image of abstinence, simplicity, and devotion, as the clergy had adopted black for the vestments they wore for everyday functions and certain formal ceremonies.

Black first became a proper color of fashion during the Renaissance. At that time, black dyes were extremely expensive and hard to reproduce, so the color was worn only by members of the aristocratic class. It was therefore rightfully viewed as a badge of authority for the powers that be, but also as a synonym of piety—an image that society's leaders were at great pains to project, to protect themselves from insurrections instigated by the masses.

Starting in the 16th century, in opposition to the increasingly extravagant splendor of the European courts, with their bling-bling gold and silver lamés, the Spanish royalty opted for black, with its formal restraint and austerity. Yet this position was also somewhat deceptive, in that black, considered to be the ultimate color of humility, perfectly set off the costly white lace that adorned the collars and cuffs of the nobles, and intensified the gleam and munificence of their spectacular jewels.

Black's popularity as a power color would then wane until the 19th century, when it made its comeback in the fashion world. This renewed interest was due to the development of chemical dyes, which could reproduce the color at a far lower cost and on a far larger scale than in the past. At the same time, the rules of dress associated with the loss of a dearly beloved became codified and structured, with distinctions between full mourning and half mourning, the latter characterized by a gradual return to color. The rules governing mourning were some of the most elaborate in the etiquette books of the era, and women's magazines published frequent articles on the subject, complete with complex definitions and time periods (18 months for widows) that made black commonplace on women. Yet mourning was not incompatible with coquetry, and fashion magazines kept their readers abreast of the latest styles and fabrics. Toward the end of the century, once the full mourning period was over, it became difficult to distinguish a mourning dress from something that was simply lovely, and black. In 1894, the magazine *La Mode Illustrée* explained this inevitable phenomenon: "We pared down the duration, then the severity of the various mourning periods; and precisely because it would have been indecent to go to the theater, to attend races, dinners, and meetings wearing the uniform of full mourning, it gradually transformed, and from severe has become very nearly attractive… so that the mourning dress is often nothing more than an elegant black outfit."

Black evening dresses were considered to be ultra-sophisticated and extremely glamorous, as they reinforced the beauty of the white skin that was so highly prized at this time. Worn by both respectable women and courtesans alike, black robes were disturbing, and exerted a sensual fascination on the minds of men. This was exemplified by the full standing portrait of "Madame X" by American painter John Singer Sargent, which scandalized Parisian society when it was shown at the 1884 Salon des Beaux-Arts, as its approach was unacceptably sexual for the period. The first version of the painting featured a strap that had ingenuously "slipped" from Madame X's shoulder to her bared arm, thereby accentuating the total nudity of her plunging neckline. It was too much for the public, which nonetheless flocked en masse to the disparaged painting. Sargent eventually repainted the strap to its rightful place. But the damage was done, adding to the sulfurous, even obscene reputation of black finery.

In the early 20th century, black was also in fashion, albeit unintentionally: World War I had created so many widows that it became the dominant color in a woman's wardrobe. But it wasn't until 1923 that the modern, fashionable little black dress went mass. This was when the modestly sized Parisian fashion house Premet proposed "a little slip of a frock," dubbed "La Garçonne," in homage to the bestselling book by French writer Victor Margueritte. This dress was tremendously successful and became a virtual archetype of the emancipated woman. Between authorized reproductions and counterfeit copies, one million Garçonne dresses were sold around the world.

The process came full circle three years later with Gabrielle Chanel and what *Vogue* referred to as "the frock that all the world will wear." With her interpretation of the little black dress, Mademoiselle Chanel synthesized the modernity and the major upheavals of the Roaring Twenties. She thereby cemented the fame of the dress in question, which was adopted overwhelmingly on both sides of the Atlantic.

During the 1930s, Hollywood deployed its wiles with film noir, a genre that defined the concept of glamour, incarnated by *femmes fatales* draped in bewitching black dresses. These dresses, like the stars who wore them, soon acquired iconic status and entered into the pantheon of the feminine ideal: Marlene Dietrich in *Shanghai Express*, Joan Crawford in *Possessed* and *Grand Hotel*, and Greta Garbo in *Mata Hari*.

Simultaneously, in Europe, the Spanish designer Cristóbal Balenciaga interpreted this purity with an elegance that became legendary. As *Harper's Bazaar* described it in 1938: "His black is so black that it gives you the chills. It's a deep, Spanish, nearly velvety black, a starless night, a black that makes almost any other ordinary black turn to gray." Endowed with an incomparable savoir-faire and science of proportions, Balenciaga enshrined this color, propelling it to the pinnacle of distinction and refinement.

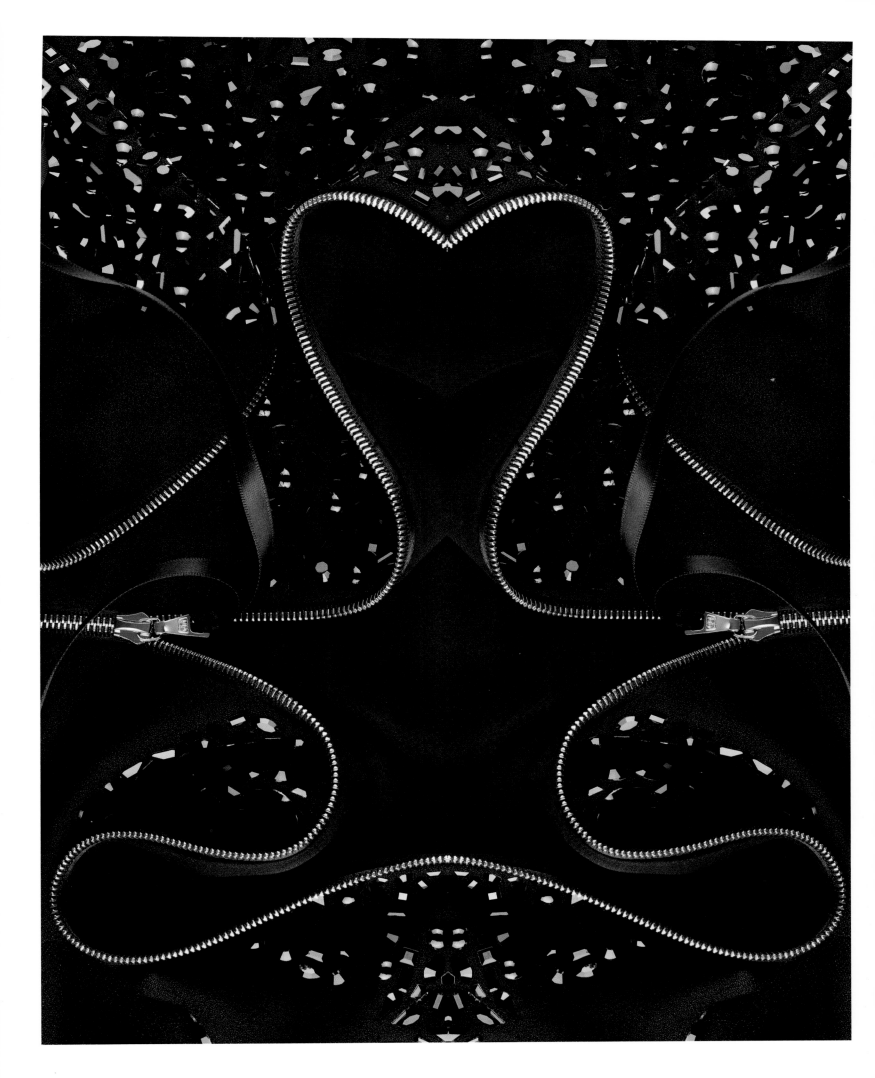

Just after World War II, Christian Dior broke decisively with the prevalent military style of the preceding years, crystallizing the new aesthetic of a revived femininity that earned him the rank of "dictator of style." He treated black as a basic that encapsulated a woman's silhouette marvelously, bringing out her body while setting off his construction and shapes. "You can wear black at any time. You can wear it at any age. You may wear it on almost any occasion. A 'little black frock' is essential to a woman's wardrobe. I could write a book about black…" From this point on, the black dress had become a dependable, highly prized item.

Yves Saint Laurent, the direct heir of Christian Dior, discussed the subject clearly, in 1990, looking back over the dawn of his career: "Black was the expression of my first collections, thick black marks that symbolized the line of the pencil on the white page: the silhouette at the peak of its purity."

The constantly changing use of black has been bolstered by elements from every culture, including rock'n'roll and its black leather jackets, and later, the accoutrements of the English punks, whose black clothes were plastered with provocative slogans. In fashion, it was the Japanese who in 1981 made headlines by deconstructing the body's shape in black, in the process creating a new definition of beauty. Rei Kawakubo for Comme des Garçons and Yohji Yamamoto used black as the cornerstone of their designs. It not only determined their chromatic palettes, but it was an ambience, a metaphor, a philosophy. According to Yamamoto: "Black signals a difference. It's in opposition to the streets of my country's cities, which sparkle with vibrant, irritating colors. Black is a requirement. It's tranquility, rest, the minimal gestures of the Noh theater, as opposed to Kabuki, which consists of colors…"

Through all these metamorphoses, the stylistic vocabulary of the little black dress has constantly expanded so that today, a plethora of possibilities exists. Glamorous or modest, alluring or functional, elegant or chic, modern or classic, discreet or flashy, the little black dress expresses an extensive and sophisticated language, which evokes every possible option, exactly like the color it uses. Worn day or night, it is the perfect backdrop allowing a woman to express the multiple facets of her personality.

As an emblem that is recognizable and unique among all the current dress codes, the little black dress is a major, recurring theme, and any worthy wardrobe must have one. Over the centuries, it has transformed and evolved with changing whims, while remaining a basic. This gives it its unique status as dependable and all-purpose, and is surely the reason for its unfailing success story. Still remarkably popular, the dress remains a mainstay thanks to the fashion designers who offer these unique versions, as if perfecting an eternal exercise in style.

Pamela Golbin

Curator-in-chief, Fashion and Textile Collection at Les Arts Décoratifs, Louvre Paris

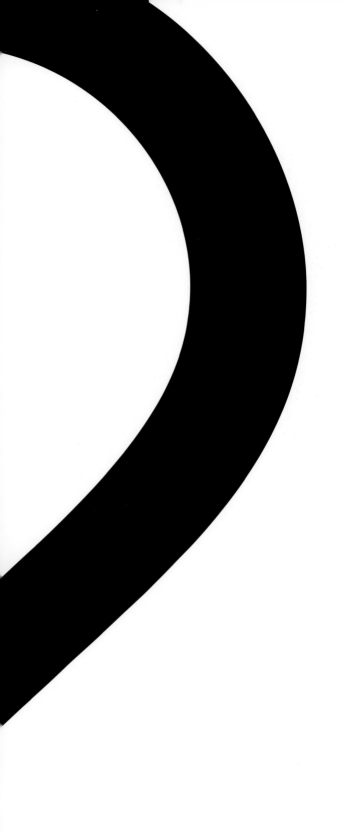

ways to say **black**

3.1 PHILLIP LIM 01

Picasso's cubist collages were the inspiration behind American designer Phillip Lim's crystal-embellished duchesse satin shift. The 2007 winner of the CFDA Swarovski Award for emerging talent in Womenswear explains that he chose a classic shape, but optically fractured it with a collage of hand-selected Jet-colored SWAROVSKI ELEMENTS, which were stitched onto black patches set against an ivory satin backdrop to create the illusion that they were floating in air. "I am drawn to the delicate difference between surface textures," Lim says. "I wanted to explore that tension by making it look as if these shapes were suspended and merging."

For such a relatively young designer, Lim, 35, has experienced a string of successes. He started his career as a design assistant at the chic sportswear company Katayone Adeli and then co-created the sharp, minimalist label Development in 2000. When Lim debuted his 3.1 phillip lim line in 2005 (named in part for his and business partner Wen Zhou's shared age at the time—31), its offbeat elegance made it an instant favorite with critics, celebrities, and fashion editors. Lim sees his line as producing "beautiful clothes with added touches of madness, striving toward the imperfection." 3.1 phillip lim is available in 45 countries and carried in nearly 400 boutiques and department stores worldwide including four flagship stores in New York, Los Angeles, Tokyo, and Seoul.

PHOTOGRAPHY Scheltens & Abbenes

02 ALBERTA FERRETTI

"The little black dress has become an icon, able to transform nothing into something chic," says Alberta Ferretti, a designer who is an expert on the art and science of the dress. This silk chiffon frock, which Ferretti created at her studio in the hamlet of Cattolica, Italy, is shaped by a corset set with various different cuts of Jet-colored SWAROVSKI ELEMENTS to evoke a piece of jewelry. The fabric trails off the bodice, resulting in a dynamic silhouette. "A little suggestion," cautions Ferretti. "I would wear it without jewels."

Ferretti has long created preciously adorned, romantic clothes, with a particular fondness for beading, tucking, twisting, and goddess-like draping. Since she launched her collection in 1993, and followed with her second line, Philosophy di Alberta Ferretti, in 1998, Ferretti has earned such admirers as Meryl Streep, Drew Barrymore, and Scarlett Johansson. Today, she operates 35 freestanding retail stores in locations ranging from Abu Dhabi to Taipei, and her collection is featured in hundreds of department and specialty stores worldwide. Along with her brother Massimo, Ferretti owns Aeffe, a production and distribution operation representing Jean Paul Gaultier, Moschino, Authier, Velmar, and Pollini. A frequent presence at international film festivals, she is one of the truly *beau monde* of Cannes, where she often attends the annual amfAR gala with a coterie of clients.

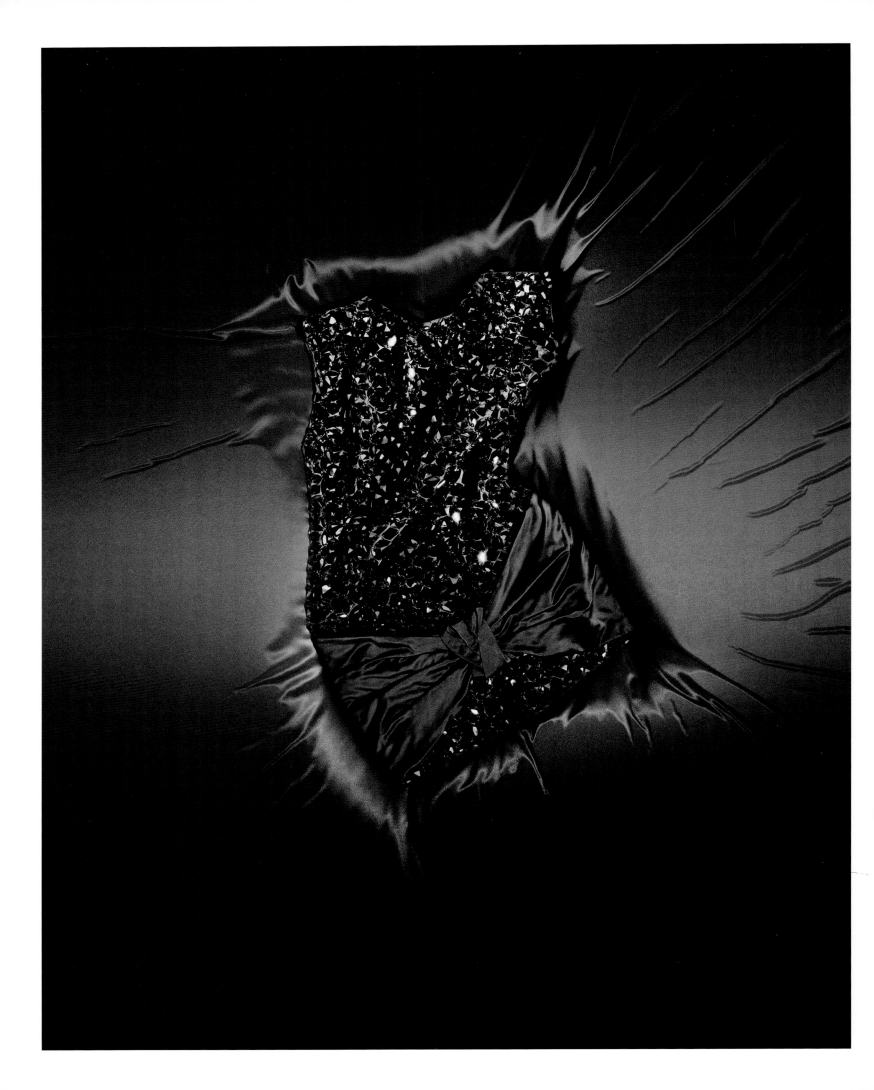

ALEXIS MABILLE 03

"I wanted to do something really evening," explains Alexis Mabille of his fanciful sleeveless shift in duchesse satin, embellished with SWAROVSKI ELEMENTS. "I thought it would be interesting to create a very geometrical, futuristic shape and cover it in crystal scales, like python or crocodile." His final effort contains an extraordinary amount of handcrafting, with three days spent to execute the embroidery alone.

A veteran of Dior and YSL, Mabille has only shown his own collection for the last four years, but he has rapidly become known as one of Paris's most dynamic young designers, attracting such fans as Keira Knightley and Carla Bruni-Sarkozy. A native of Lyon, he spent his childhood piecing together garments found in museums and attics, and created costumes and clothes for family and friends during his teenage years. Mabille earned his diploma from the Chambre Syndicale de la Couture Parisienne in 1997, and after apprenticing at Ungaro and Nina Ricci, he joined the design team at Christian Dior, working on fine jewelry under John Galliano and for Hedi Slimane's Dior Homme. After nine years at the house, he launched his ALEXIS MABILLE collection of daring unisex ready-to-wear that combines sensuous fabrics, sharp tailoring, and dandyish adornment such as bow ties.

04 AZZARO

"I really love to doodle shadows when sketching," explains Azzaro's creative director Vanessa Seward. "For this dress, my inspiration was a black-and-white drawing, with different shades of crystals representing the shadows found in a sketch." Seward began with wool crepe, one of the materials she uses most for Azzaro's feminine clothes, and added 1,500 SWAROVSKI ELEMENTS in hues ranging from black to translucent to create a trompe-l'œil effect. The end result, after 80 hours of embroidery finished with silver thread, is an elegantly draped mini-dress anchored by an alluring bustier.

Ever since 2004, when Seward relaunched the French house after Loris Azzaro's death, it has become the go-to creator of statement party frocks evocative of another, more glamorous era. An aficionado of SWAROVSKI ELEMENTS, Seward often uses them as buttons running up the back of a dress or to punctuate a long sleeve. She frequently collaborates with artists and musicians on Azzaro's collections, and now she has created an alter ego out of her sleek little white cat, Monsieur Jo, whose crystal likeness skips across dresses and jackets.

A native of Argentina, Seward was raised in London, Paris, and Buenos Aires before becoming an assistant, at age 21, to Karl Lagerfeld at Chanel. Today, she operates out of a studio on top of the boutique at the rue du Faubourg Saint Honoré, and is known to host salon-like events with her husband, the music producer Bertrand Burgalat. A film aficionado, she has also enjoyed some screen time in *2 Days in Paris*, which was written and directed by her longtime friend, Julie Delpy.

BOUDICCA 05

Zowie Broach and Brian Kirkby, the duo behind the British couture and prêt-à-porter label Boudicca, began as fine artists, exhibiting severely tailored, imaginatively proportioned clothing in galleries. By 2003, they had spread out onto runways, too, thanks in part to a sponsorship from American Express that allowed for the expansion.

For their contribution to the 22 Ways to Say Black initiative, Broach and Kirkby returned to their roots, designing a resin mannequin that was ultimately rendered by the Royal College of Art in London. Encased in a Victorian-style glass dome, it wears a miniature version of their "Tornado Dress." Every element of the piece was handcrafted, including the application of tiny SWAROVSKI ELEMENTS in color Jet on the black netting and the placement of self-adhesive Crystal-it motifs on the paper flooring to mimic spots of black ink.

Named for the Celtic rebel queen who led a revolt against the Roman Empire and burned London to the ground, Boudicca is infused with a radical spirit that has carried through to the house's first fragrance. Launched in 2008, Wode comes bottled in a graffiti can, and mists on blue before disappearing onto the skin, emulating for a moment the blue war paint that Boudicca herself wore into battle.

06 CATHERINE MALANDRINO

The Grenoble-born, New York-based designer Catherine Malandrino has become one of the loveliest standard-bearers of fashionable insouciance. She creates clothes that she says are "ultra-feminine, comfortable, edgy, and with a touch of humor." With aesthetics inspired by "the craftsmanship, draping, and sewing of French couture, and the vibrant energy of the streets of New York," Malandrino created an exemplar in this "bubbling little black dress for night owls." The cashmere shift, worn over a beige slip, is made with an intricate, wrap-hoop technique that sets off an abundance of large-scaled SWAROVSKI ELEMENTS in multiple colors like Crystal, Crystal Tabac, Olivine, Black Diamond, and Jet.

Malandrino began her career in Paris working in the houses of such fashion innovators as Louis Féraud and Emanuel Ungaro, and, in the 1990s, became the creative force behind the French label Et Vous. In 1998 she debuted her own company in New York City, which today consists of her contemporary Catherine Malandrino line and a luxury collection called Malandrino. Her iconic flag dress, which debuted in 2000, has become a favorite of such women as Halle Berry, Julia Roberts, Madonna, and Zandra Rhodes, whose Fashion and Textile Museum in London currently has the dress on display. And Malandrino recently added another position to her resume, television personality, thanks to her acclaimed role as a judge during season two of the Bravo Network reality show *Make Me a Supermodel*.

DIANE VON FURSTENBERG 07

This sundial-pleated dress with a silk and double-faced satin belt features a vast amount of intricate crystal detailing: the design on the open-lattice-work sleeves, which was based on a motif featured in the Power Ring for her fine jewelry collection DvF by H Stern, contains approximately 500 SWAROVSKI ELEMENTS in shades of Jet Hematite, Jet, and Crystal on each arm; on the belt are an additional 400. Inspired by her love of *femmes fatales* such as Marlene Dietrich, von Furstenberg's goal was to mix 1940s Hollywood glamour with the ease and functionality of her iconic wrap dress, the radically original design that launched her career in 1972. A success almost overnight, von Furstenberg was recognized as an innovator with a unique understanding of how to flatter a woman's body—so much so that *Newsweek* proclaimed her "the most marketable designer since Coco Chanel" in a 1976 cover story. That moniker proved to be well deserved, as today von Furstenberg is still a titan in the fashion industry, both as a top designer and the president of the Council of Fashion Designers of America. Currently, her clothes and accessories are sold in over 56 countries, including in her 29 freestanding Diane von Furstenberg boutiques in major cities including New York, Los Angeles, Miami, London, Paris, Moscow, and Tokyo.

08 DONNA KARAN NEW YORK

The internationally-renowned American designer Donna Karan employed 23 seamstresses to attach the 2,600 dramatic sew-on stones and pendants on this floor-length viscose jersey gown. A shimmering mass of SWAROVSKI ELEMENTS in tones of Crystal, Crystal Silver Shade, Black Diamond and Jet seems to explode over the draped neckline like breathtaking Magellanic Clouds, the companion galaxies of the Milky Way that Karan had in mind when creating the piece. Along with the dignity and simplicity that have become a Karan signature, another of her stylistic hallmarks is represented in this dress: the masterful use of black, which she has developed since the beginning of her career.

Karan is the daughter of a custom tailor and a showroom fit model, so fashion has always been a part of her life. She came to national attention in 1974, when she took the reins at Anne Klein, before launching her own label years later to wide acclaim, due in large part to the brilliance of her "Seven Easy Pieces." These were universally flattering, mix-and-match separates offered in a trend-setting, all-black palette. From there, her company continued to grow, encompassing beauty and home collections, accessories, denim, and multiple ready-to-wear lines. Deservedly lauded for having shifted fashion towards what real women need and desire, Karan has received recognition from the Council of Fashion Designers; she won the Fashion Group International Superstar Award in 2003 and was named a *Glamour* magazine Woman of the Year in 2007. "Everything is a matter of body and soul," Karan says. "For me, designing is an expression of who I am as a woman with all the feelings, complications and emotions."

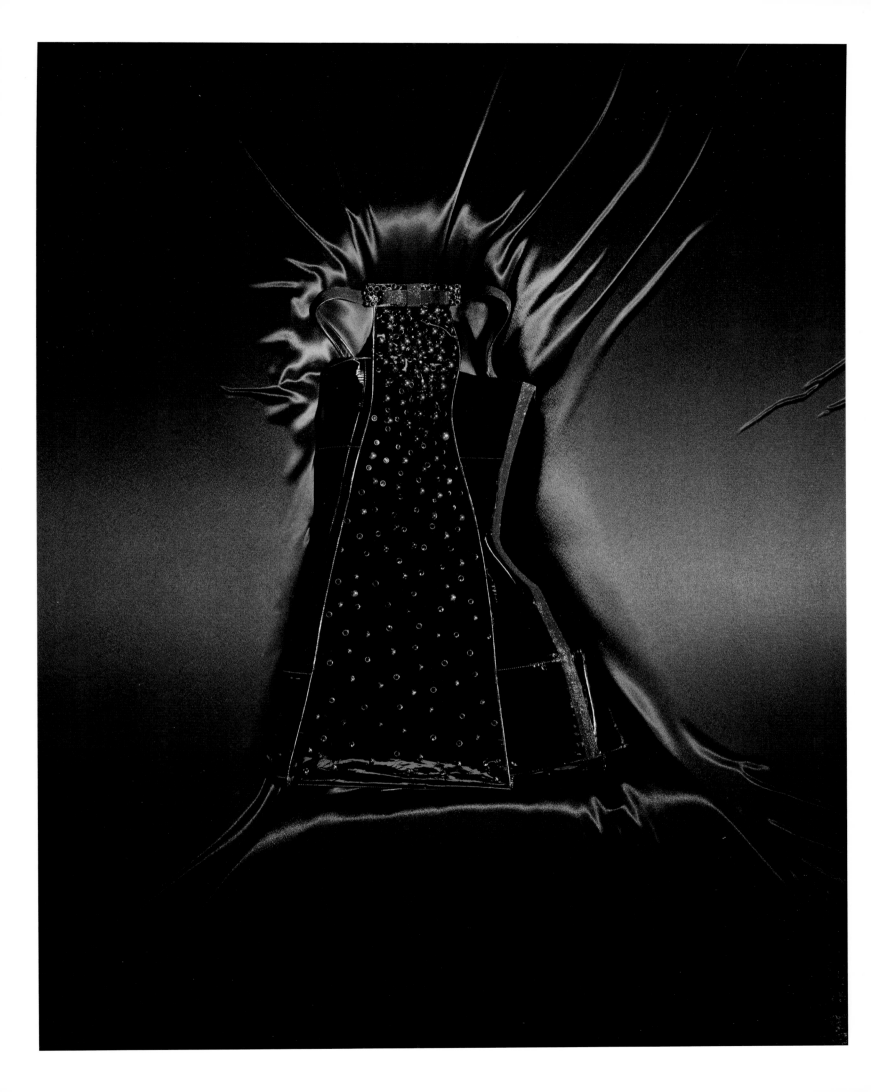

FENDI 09

Under the guidance of creative director Karl Lagerfeld, Fendi's design team formed this graphic apron dress out of patent nappa sheepskin. The A-line silhouette is enhanced by cleverly placed front and back panels, embellished by Crystal Rivets and Crystal Pearls to add extra shine. Other clever details include straps and a side beam trimmed with Crystal Fabric in Jet Hematite and a feminine finishing touch: two bows, one entirely covered by Jet-colored Crystal Rivets.

Though today Fendi is known as an entirely contemporary brand, the company has a long heritage. Founded in 1925 by newlyweds Adele and Edoardo Fendi as the expansion of a business started by Adele in 1918, what began as a small leather and fur company on Rome's Via del Plebiscito has expanded through the years into an industry that, by the 1940s, included all five of the couple's daughters. In 1966, Lagerfeld came on board, and immediately created the "Double-F" logo that has since become an international sensation. In 1969, Fendi first showed prêt-à-porter furs in Florence, designed, unusually at the time, to connect with their evolving leather accessories. Ready-to-wear fashion followed in 1977, and in the next decade, was joined by denim, ties, gloves, sunglasses, home goods, and more. In the mid-1990s Fendi's appeal reached truly global levels, thanks to the Baguette bag launched by Silvia Venturini Fendi in the winter season of 1997/98. Seemingly overnight, the category of "It Bag" was born. In time for its 80th anniversary in 2005, the company opened the Palazzo Fendi flagship in Rome, which houses the corporate headquarters, the fur studio, and the largest Fendi boutique in the world. And two years later, Fendi went where no fashion house had gone before, staging a runway presentation on the Great Wall of China that has since gone down in history as one of the industry's most memorable moments.

10 GASPARD YURKIEVICH

"My idea was to use something very substantial, like metal and crystal, to create the ruffles," explains the Paris-based designer Gaspard Yurkievich of this fanciful cocktail dress made of Crystal Aerial Mesh with Jet-colored crystals in golden casings. "It required a lot of hand work, but that was what interested me, to do something that I don't do in my prêt-à-porter collection."

In the 11 years since Yurkievich founded his eponymous line, he has become a cult favorite for his whimsical, edgy interpretation of Parisian chic. Born and raised in France's capital city, he studied fashion at the Studio Berçot and, upon graduation in 1993, worked for such influential figures as Jean Paul Gaultier, Thierry Mugler, and Jean Colonna. The 37-year-old designer has now united his accessories collections and men's and women's lines at a flagship boutique on rue Charlot in the Marais, which has become the neighborhood of choice for fashion independents. Thanks to his predilection for bold silhouettes, dramatic dimensions, and bright patterns, Yurkievich is often described as avant-garde, although his flattering shapes have found plenty of fans looking for a fresh take on sportswear. Yurkievich often adds a signature flourish, which, in this case, is the mesh headpiece consisting of small Jet-colored SWAROVSKI ELEMENTS in golden casings. "It references an army from the Middle Ages," explains Yurkievich, who worked with a similar concept in a previous collection. "You don't see the eyes of the person who wears it, but that person can see everything. My idea was only to see the mouth singing, This piece really rocks!" This sort of wry, inside joke is signature Yurkievich—and the reason his creations are collected so fervently.

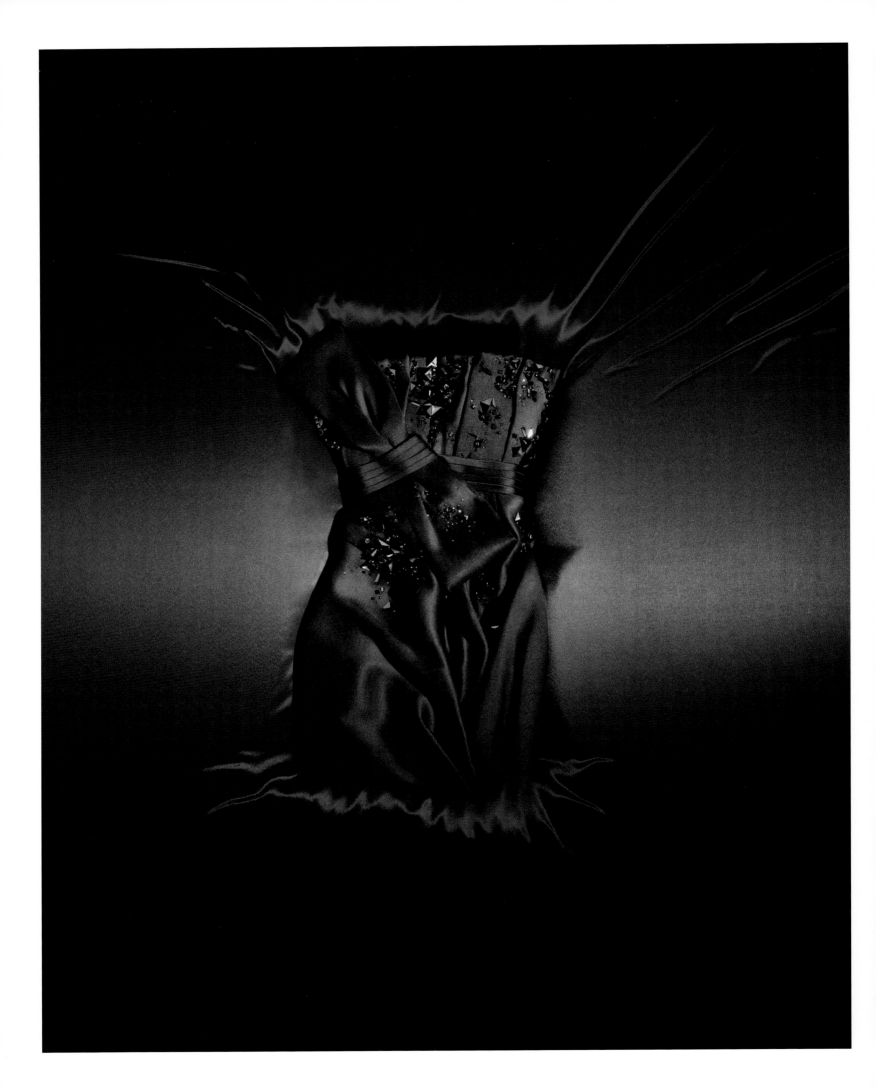

GIANFRANCO FERRÉ 11

To inspire their strapless mini-dress, Gianfranco Ferré's new co-creative directors Tommaso Aquilano and Roberto Rimondi looked to the heavens—specifically, the phenomenon around the polar regions known as Aurora Borealis, which infuses the night sky with a faint, pastel glow. "The iridescent colors of SWAROVSKI ELEMENTS and the movement created by the draping of the dress make a similar optical effect," the designers explain of the richly embroidered and adorned piece, made of silk gazar and duchesse satin with velvet inserts.

Aquilano and Rimondi were only appointed to head Gianfranco Ferré in 2008, but they have spent over 20 years working together to craft classically inspired, form-hugging suits and dresses. Their partnership began at MaxMara, where they honed their tailoring expertise, and grew into the label 6267 in 2005, where Aquilano and Rimondi's striking silhouettes in graphic palettes of black, white, and neutral beige earned them such admirers as Jennifer Lopez, Reese Witherspoon, and Renée Zellweger.

With a special focus on fabric innovation, the duo has modernized the house of Ferré following the passing of its founder, Gianfranco Ferré, in 2007. Widely regarded as two of Italy's most exciting designers working today, Aquilano and Rimondi have cultivated a new group of fans for Ferré, including Anne Hathaway and Alicia Keys.

12 GIORGIO ARMANI PRIVÉ

"By using SWAROVSKI ELEMENTS, I was able to play with light and create a shimmering effect on moving cloth," says Giorgio Armani of this Giorgio Armani Privé couture gown. "One of the ideas that I was working with was the notion of capturing attention, not through showing flesh, but through the sculpted form of fabric. By using crystals I was able to draw attention to the contours and cut of the garments, making the wearer literally shine as she moves."

For the last 35 years, the Armani name has been synonymous with Italian fashion. What began in a small studio in Milan has been transformed into a global brand with three major ready-to-wear brands, Giorgio Armani, Armani Collezioni, and Emporio Armani, as well as a couture collection (Giorgio Armani Privé) and a contemporary brand (A/X Armani Exchange). Armani Jeans, Armani Junior, Armani Casa, Armani Hotels, and Armani Cosmetics round out a portfolio that has become the envy of all its competitors. (In 2005, *Forbes* estimated the value of Giorgio Armani's companies to be $5.2 billion.) As the first fashion house to actively dress celebrities, Armani outfitted Richard Gere in the 1980 film *American Gigolo* and has gone on to dress many others, from Cate Blanchett and David and Victoria Beckham to, most recently, Megan Fox. Additionally, Armani became only the second Italian fashion house to show during the Paris couture shows. "Couture is the purest expression of a designer's art," Armani notes. "It is an opportunity to really explore the possibilities of fashion without commercial constraints. The Giorgio Armani Privé couture line encourages customers to dream, and we believe there is always a place for dreaming in fashion."

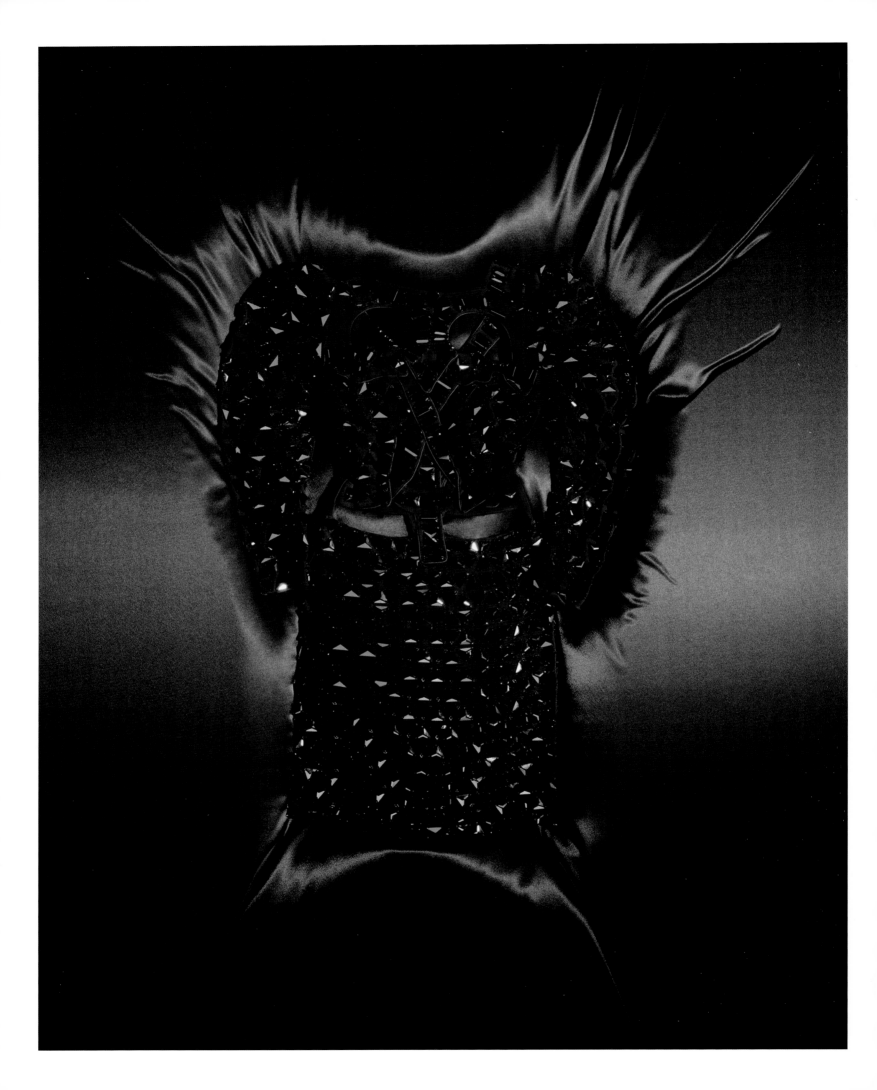

GIVENCHY BY RICCARDO TISCI 13

Few fashion houses are as famous for their little black dresses as Givenchy. Founder Hubert de Givenchy pioneered this particular art form on icons like Audrey Hepburn and Jacqueline Kennedy, and since 2005, Givenchy's creative director Riccardo Tisci has followed in his footsteps with such fans as Madonna. "The little black dress remains to this day one of Givenchy's most important and recognized codes," Tisci says. This one was inspired by the graphic quality of 1960s couture and the geometric cuts of the traditional cowboy jacket. "The severity of the overlapping 'bondage' straps adds a dark sensuality to the dress," Tisci notes. "I was looking at photos of cowboys throughout history and how they customized their jackets and shirts with jeweled brooches or medallions. To translate this, I used my favorite Jet-colored SWAROVSKI ELEMENTS applied in lines that follow the contours of the body."

Tisci's gothic-tinged romanticism, which looks to far-flung inspirations ranging from nautical knotting to the hidden glamour of Berber tribes, has won him most favored designer status among a growing number of dedicated fashion lovers. Born in Como, Italy, Tisci graduated from London's Central Saint Martins in 1999 and worked in relative obscurity until showing his first eponymous collection in Milan in 2004. The following year he was discovered, anointed creative director at Givenchy, and promptly set out to restore the house to its golden age of creativity. One of the hottest tickets during Paris Fashion Week, Tisci also creates two haute couture collections a year.

14 JEAN PAUL GAULTIER

"Working on a little black dress is never easy," explains Jean Paul Gaultier. "How to make this classic contemporary?" For Gaultier that was achieved with the "X" motif that he has also explored in his Fall/Winter 2009/10 collection. Made of silk taffeta and secured by shoulder straps, the large "X," made of Jet-colored SWAROVSKI ELEMENTS, is what Gaultier calls "couture calligraphy," offset by alluring organza peek-a-boo panels to create a graphic statement across the body.

Gaultier has been an international fashion force since 1976, when he released his first independent collection after working for Pierre Cardin and Jean Patou. Hailing from Arcueil in the Val-de-Marne, he had no formal training but he quickly emerged as the industry's *enfant terrible*—a term still used to describe him. A pioneer of exuberant runway shows and an advocate of unbridled creativity, Gaultier draws inspiration from everywhere: streets, museums, abroad. His haute couture line, Gaultier Paris, is one of the best-selling of the Chambre Syndicale's remaining 11 recognized practitioners of the art, and his shows are frequently jammed with celebrities ranging from Catherine Deneuve to Kylie Minogue. Gaultier also currently serves as the creative director of Hermès, for which he consistently earns critical kudos and admirable sales.

"I have used SWAROVSKI ELEMENTS in my designs many times," notes the designer. "They enable me to show my vision even more clearly—or should I say sparkly?"

LANVIN BY ALBER ELBAZ 15

At the head of a house known for its endlessly charming ways to render a dress, Lanvin's designer Alber Elbaz has relished the opportunity to incorporate a trompe-l'œil twist into this one with SWAROVSKI ELEMENTS. Elbaz went beyond mere adornment here, explaining that the crystals he used were "a part of the construction of the dress, not just decoration. They are suspended within the dress, rather than merely sitting on top of it like a necklace." Ten meters of bias-cut satin bands, treated with a scarf-finishing technique, and touches of tulle add recognizable elements of Elbaz's signature whimsy.

The Moroccan-born, Paris-based designer was named the artistic director of Lanvin in 2001 after serving at Geoffrey Beene, Guy Laroche, and Yves Saint Laurent Rive Gauche. Under his initiative, the house known for elegant ready-to-wear in the 1920s and 1930s under its founder, Jeanne Lanvin, has become a touchstone of modern fashion the world over. Elbaz's wearable, but highly original daywear consistently earns critical raves, and red-carpet habitués like Natalie Portman and Tilda Swinton rely on Lanvin during awards season as well. With an ardent following among the fashion media, Lanvin's runway presentations have become some of the most-watched in fashion, with clothes that are endlessly referenced but impossible to copy.

16 MARIOS SCHWAB

"Black requires a well-balanced silhouette," explains Marios Schwab. "It all rests on the cut and the type of adornment, as black absorbs detail." For his molded cocktail shift, "The Little Black Bustle Dress," Schwab created a peek-a-boo slice encrusted with various sizes of SWAROVSKI ELEMENTS, to embody a precious "secret world of underneath a Victorian bustle," he says. "It is an element of the unexpected, making a play of 'hide and reveal' out of certain lines of the body."

A graduate of Berlin's Esmod fashion school, where he won the Best Student Award, Schwab moved to London in 2003 and completed his Master's Degree in Fashion specializing in womenswear at Central Saint Martins College of Art and Design. Within four years, Schwab was named Best New Designer at the British Fashion Awards, and won the coveted Swiss Textiles Foundation's Stella Contemporary Fashion Award in recognition of his exceptional use and development of fabrics.

Schwab's ability to make rigid construction fluidly feminine has earned him such fans as Chloë Sevigny, Kate Moss, Christina Ricci, and Diane Kruger. Rounding out his growing resume, in May 2009 Schwab was named creative director of Halston, and unveils his first collection for the brand during New York Fashion Week in February 2010.

MARTIN GRANT 17

"I wanted the dress to have some nuance," says Martin Grant of his creation, which is entirely covered with crystals that have been arranged in a faded, ombré pattern. "The shape is very simple, with slightly exaggerated hips and shoulders. But I was rather attracted by the look of *galuchat*, or stingray skin, and its reptilian quality." To achieve that effect, Grant applied SWAROVSKI ELEMENTS to wool and silk gazar, a structured material often used in tailored dressing from the 1950s and 1960s. "It's stiff, but not at all heavy. Rather than the crystals becoming just one part of the dress, they became its whole surface. In a way, it became like working with leather." Grant's sharp piece is rendered all the more rare because the designer so rarely strays from the angular, embellishment-free silhouettes that have made him a favorite of such stylish women as Cate Blanchett, Lauren Hutton, and Lee Radziwill.

A native of Australia, Grant launched his first ready-to-wear collection at the age of 16 in his Little Collins Street studio. Several years later, already a major star in Australia, he took a four-year break to study sculpture at the Victorian College of Arts, before wending his way to Paris in 1992, where he has stayed ever since. Maintaining an unassuming profile on the fashion circuit, Grant has nonetheless developed an ardent client base devoted to his flattering, easy-to-wear designs. His collections—including a prized line of graphic, sculptural jewelry—are sold at his freestanding boutique in the Marais in Paris as well as top department stores worldwide, including Barneys New York and Le Bon Marché.

18 MISSONI

Renowned for its luxurious, durable knits in bold, distinctive patterns, Missoni has long known how to combine comfort with elegance. This Crystal Fabric, silk, and Lurex® shift is clearly a product of the same creativity. It features an asymmetrical back fastened by three distinctive Jet Hematite-colored crystals.

Missoni the company was born in Varese, Italy, in 1958 when the husband-and-wife team of Ottavio (also known as Tai) and Rosita Missoni first presented a small fashion collection. After years of experimentation with a knitting machine in their shop in the basement of their building, the Missonis caught the influential eyes of Anna Piaggi (then the fashion editor of *Arianna*), and Diana Vreeland (then the editor of American *Vogue*). In 1967, the brand was catapulted even further into the spotlight when lightweight Missoni tops were rendered see-through under runway lighting, exposing the models' bare chests underneath. The brand took off from there, expanding over the years to include everything from perfume (launched in 1980) to home-furnishing textiles (first presented in 1983) to ancillary lines like M Missoni. In the 1990s, Rosita and Tai passed the head designing duties on to their daughter Angela. She continues to impress critics by updating the grand Missoni traditions with streamlined silhouettes and a lighter palette. "We have always believed that clothes have to last," she says.

SONIA RYKIEL 19

"Tête d'Affiche," or "Top Billing," as Sonia Rykiel dubbed her unique little black ensemble, is actually a jacket made of cotton over a dress made of extra-fine merino wool adorned with more than 150 SWAROVSKI ELEMENTS. Sonia Rykiel herself and a team of 11 staffers created the ensemble, one of the few Rykiel has ever custom-made, inspired quite simply by "Madame Rykiel and her spirit."

That spirit is formidable. A native of Paris, after six years of in-house designing for the boutique Laura, owned by her husband, Rykiel founded her own label in 1968 and set up shop on the rue de Grenelle. It took *Women's Wear Daily* almost no time to dub her the "Queen of Knitwear," as her body-hugging pullovers, often striped or emblazoned with words, perfectly captured the free spirit of the age. An outspoken nonconformist, Rykiel has since become one of French fashion's most recognizable players, both personally, with her flame-red curls, and professionally, with such innovations as the poor boy sweater and inside-out seaming.

Rykiel has since made her company a family affair, when her daughter Nathalie began producing her fashion shows in the 1980s. In 1995, Nathalie was named artistic director and managing director of the house, and she became president in 2007—just in time to throw a gala at the Parc de Saint-Cloud for the label's 40th anniversary, and a special retrospective at the Musée des Arts Décoratifs.

20 THAKOON

Thai-born American designer Thakoon Panichgul took up a theme for this cocktail shift that has recurred in much of his celebrated work: "soft bondage," as he describes it. It may seem a surprising connotation for a designer whose refined clothing has become a favorite of First Lady Michelle Obama, but Panichgul is talking about constricting and accentuating the body with strips and panels of fabric. In this original piece, he fills in the "negative space" between unadorned crepe de chine with SWAROVSKI ELEMENTS. "The end result looks like a shadow play," he says. Another detail that is becoming a signature is the exposed zipper, which Panichgul leaves uncovered to turn a constructive detail into an artistic element.

It was as recently as 2004, at the age of 29, that Panichgul launched his collection, called simply Thakoon, but critics consistently rank his success among that of more established designers, thanks in part to his understanding of the business world and his talents for predicting trends, which he honed during a four-year stint as an editor and writer at *Harper's Bazaar*. As his following continues to grow, so does his acclaim, including a nomination by the CFDA in 2007 for the Swarovski Award for Womenswear and as a 2006 recipient of the *Vogue*/CFDA Fashion Fund.

VALENTINO 21

Valentino's gifted new head designers, Maria Grazia Chiuri and Pier Paolo Piccioli, dubbed this classic shift dress "Web Couture," referring to the loom-embroidered, crystal-embellished flange that adorns the back, and which required the majority of the dress's 260 hours of production time. Chiuri and Piccioli created a virtual spider web out of Crystal Yarn, Beads, and Briolette Pendants, which is laid over a black wire structure to create "a representation of a dark fairytale," explain the designers, whose aim was to use both haute couture and prêt-à-porter techniques.

Longtime accessory designers under the house's now-retired founder, Valentino Garavani, Chiuri and Piccioli were named creative directors in 2008. While their first creations nodded to the brand's rich 45-year heritage of impeccable sportswear and luxurious gowns, the duo has more recently proposed a new direction for Valentino. For the past two seasons, they have created looks that are a bit darker, a bit softer, a bit more romantic, and a lot more individualistic. Dark and nude colors have replaced brights, but silhouettes and adornments have become compellingly delicate. This dress is very much a part of their fine-tuning. Critical reception for Chiuri and Piccioli's work has been generous, and celebrities eager to take Valentino into a new era include Evangeline Lilly, Alice Dellal, and Jennifer Aniston, who chose a beaded column by Chiuri and Piccioli for the 2009 Oscars.

22 VIVIENNE WESTWOOD

A punk icon and tailoring savant, Vivienne Westwood brings her unparalleled fabric artistry to this ruched frock, "inspired by the paintings of Mantegna," she explains. "We shot silver onto the backing of silk duchesse satin to give it a metallic sheen," and then added SWAROVSKI ELEMENTS onto an adaptable cape and peplum to create a memorable silhouette.

Westwood has been designing for almost 40 years. She first began in 1971 with her partner Malcolm McLaren, showcasing ideas at their shop on London's Kings Road which was renamed with each change of concept, from Let It Rock to Sex to World's End as it is known today. Through their shop, the pair redefine street culture with punk and subsequent collections like "Seditionaries" and "Pirates" that led to the New Romantic movement. But in 1986, Westwood shifted away from youth culture in favor of traditional Savile Row tailoring techniques, British fabrics, and 17th and 18th century art.

Today Westwood is recognized as one of the most influential fashion designers in the world. In 2004, a major retrospective of her works was shown at the Victoria and Albert Museum in London, the largest exhibition of its kind for any living British designer. It subsequently toured the world for five years and was exhibited in over ten cities. Vivienne Westwood's contribution to fashion was officially recognized when she was appointed Dame Commander of the British Empire by Her Majesty the Queen Elizabeth the Second in 2006.

"Bea

clothes *with*

touches *of*

utiful
dded
nadness"

— PHILLIP LIM

VALENTINO

GIANFRANCO FERRÉ

SONIA RYKIEL

MISSONI

LANVIN BY ALBER ELBAZ

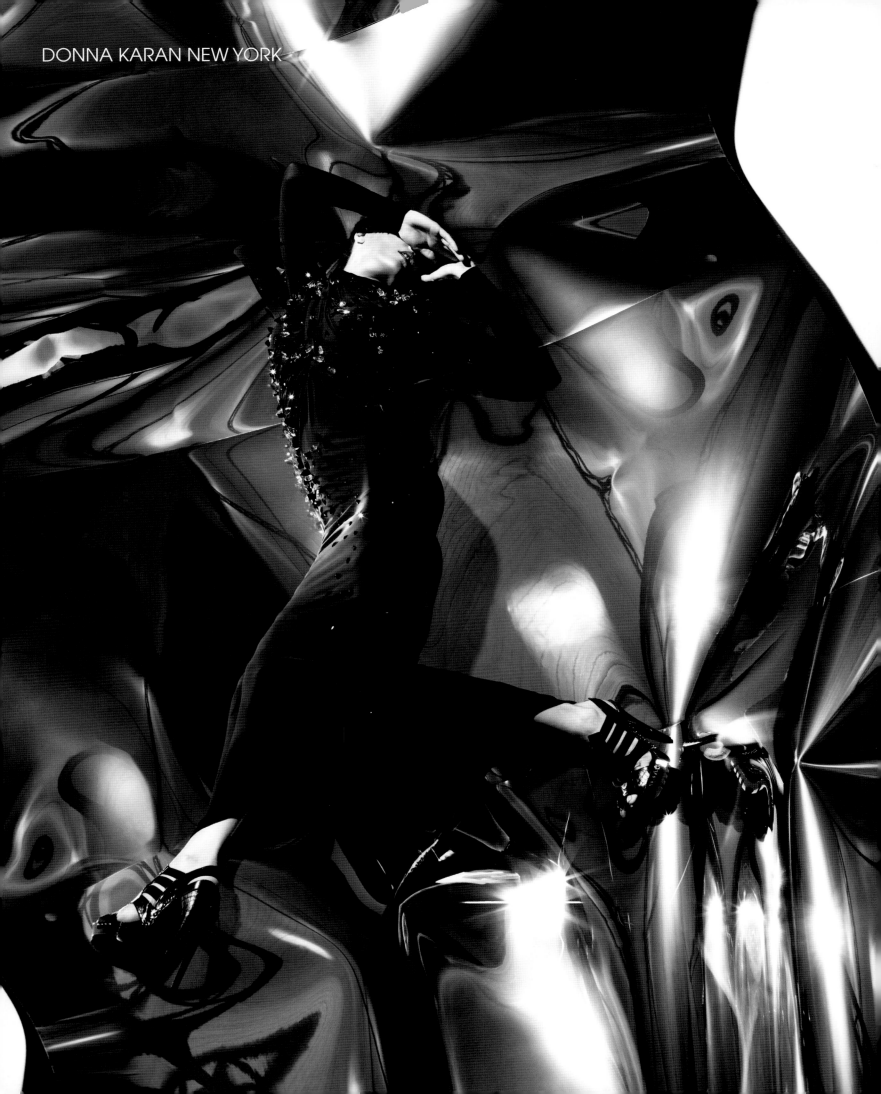

DONNA KARAN NEW YORK

GIANFRANCO FERRÉ

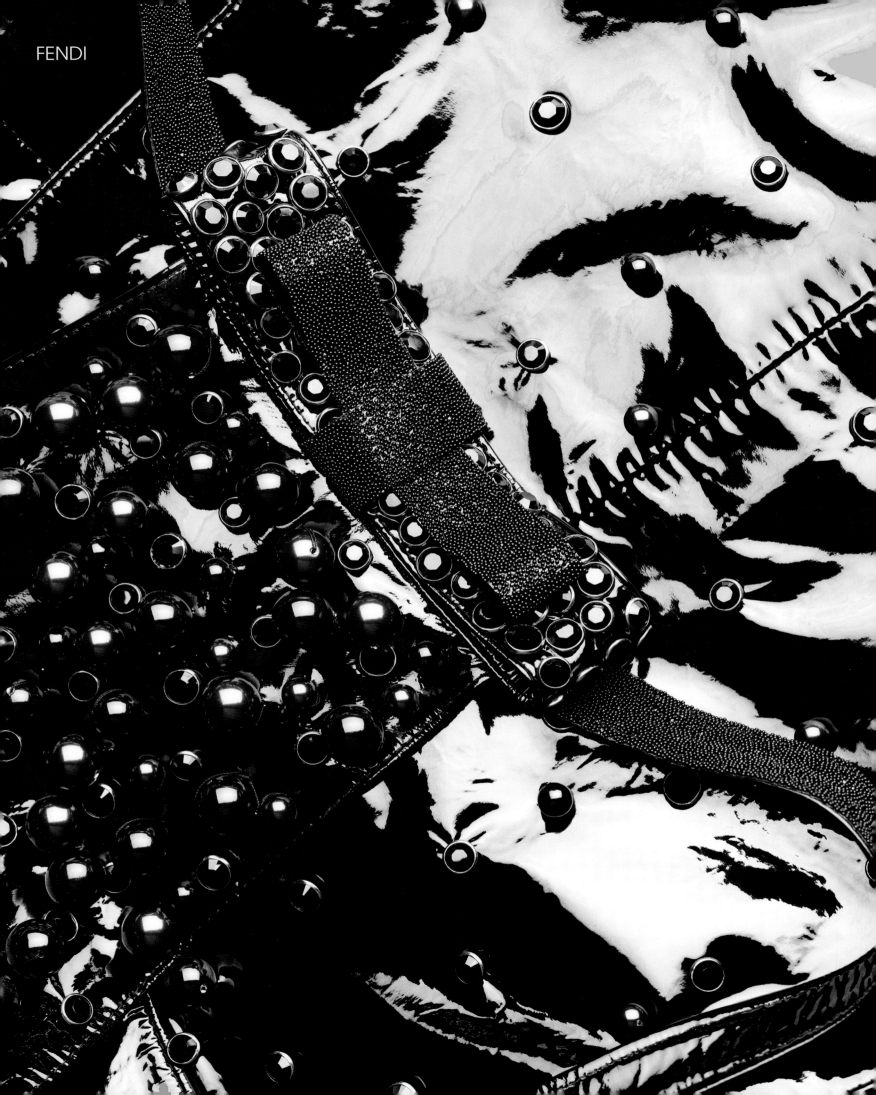

FENDI

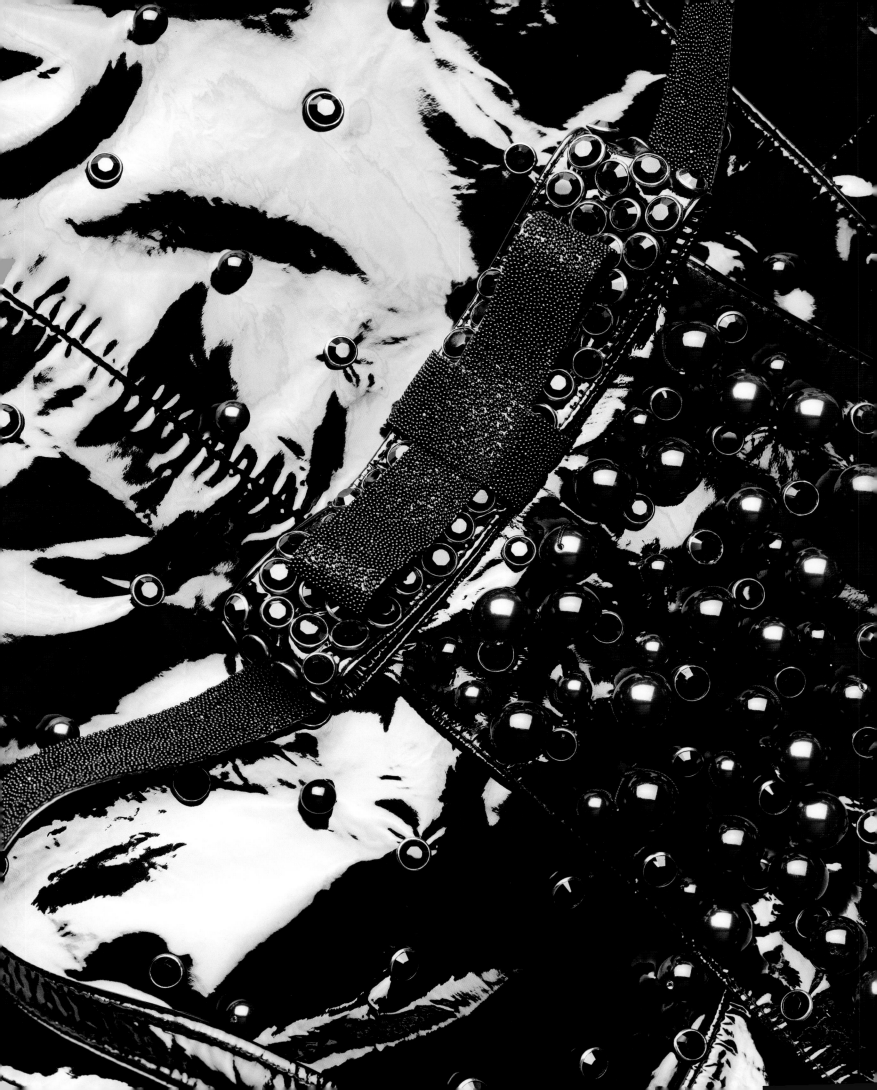

GIVENCHY BY RICCARDO TISCI

MARTIN GRANT

JEAN PAUL GAULTIER

MARIOS SCHWAB

ALEXIS MABILLE

CATHERINE MALANDRINO

GIANFRANCO FERRÉ

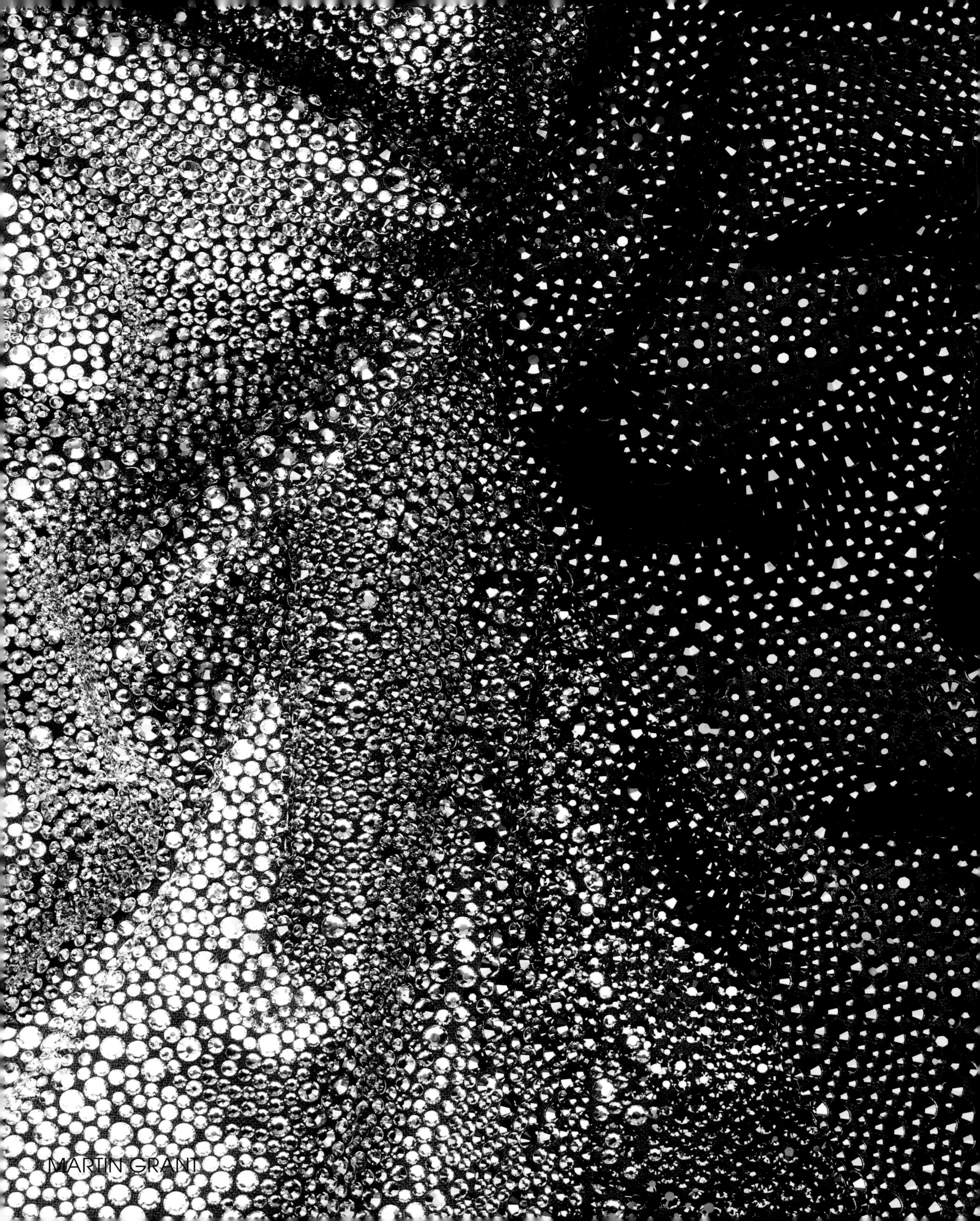
MARTIN GRANT

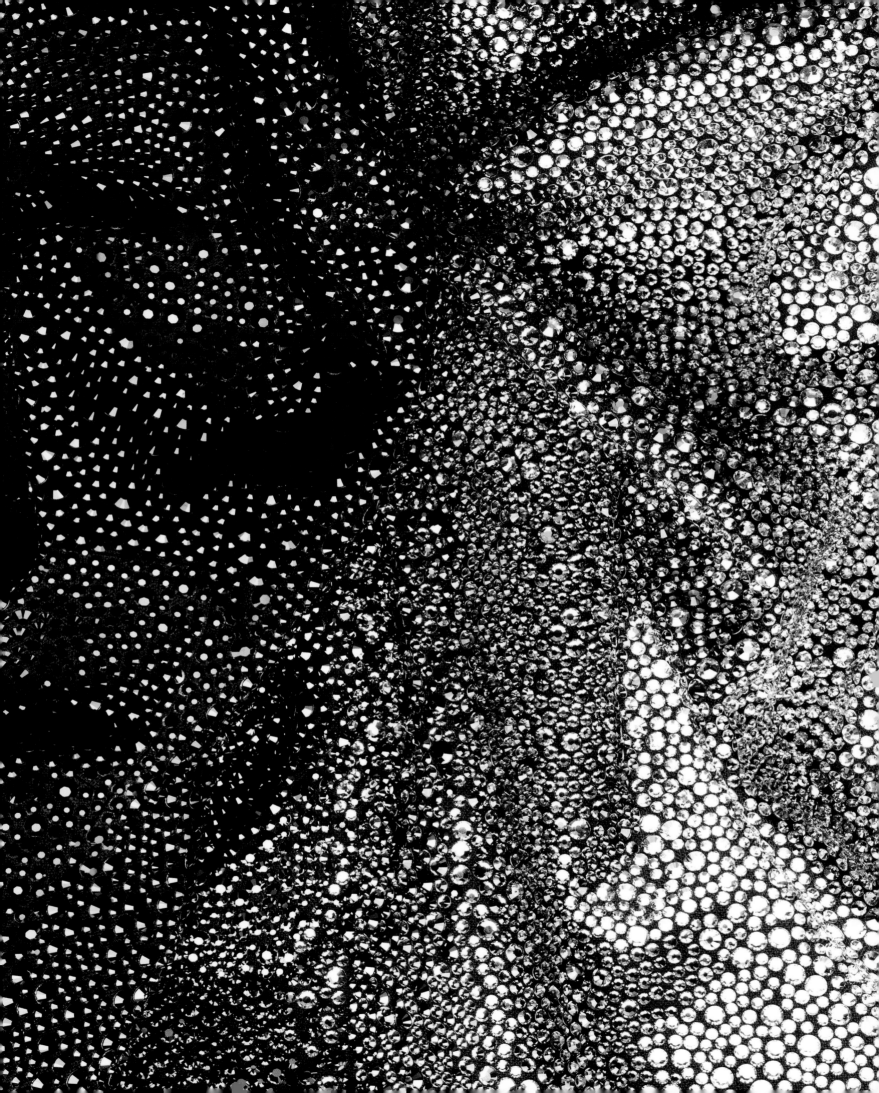

GIORGIO ARMANI PRIVÉ

GIORGIO ARMANI PRIVÉ

ALEXIS MABILLE

MARIOS SCHWAB

ALEXIS MABILLE

FENDI

ALBERTA FERRETTI

LANVIN BY ALBER ELBAZ

AZZARO

ALBERTA FERRETTI

THAKOON

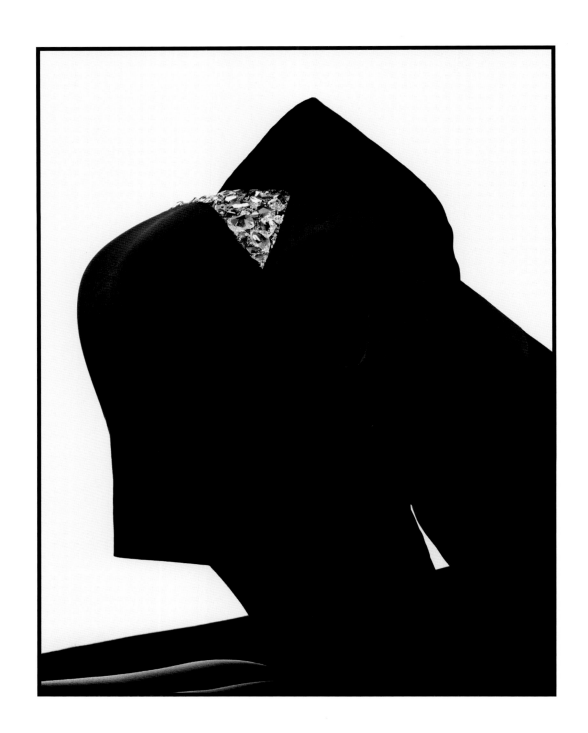

MARIOS SCHWAB

VIVIENNE WESTWOOD

VALENTINO

DIANE VON FURSTENBERG

2021 AUCTION
22 GUIDE

DESCRIPTION Sleeveless shift in ivory duchesse satin with panels in black satin and a silk charmeuse lining.

SWAROVSKI ELEMENTS
Collage of approximately 1,800 Princess Baguette, Cosmic, and Galactic Single Stone Settings, in various sizes, all in color Jet.

SIZE US 2; UK 6; France 34; Italy 36; Germany 32; Japan 5

ESTIMATE see page 132

SHOES Pierre Hardy, not included

DESCRIPTION Pleated silk chiffon mini-dress with a bodice embellished by raw-edged layered chiffon and crystals.

SWAROVSKI ELEMENTS
Hundreds of Square Lochrose, XILION Sew-on Stones, Navette, Drop, and Cosmic Baguette Sew-on Stones, all in color Jet.

SIZE US 6; UK 10; France 38; Italy 40; Germany 36; Japan 9

ESTIMATE see page 132

SHOES Pierre Hardy, not included

03 ALEXIS MABILLE

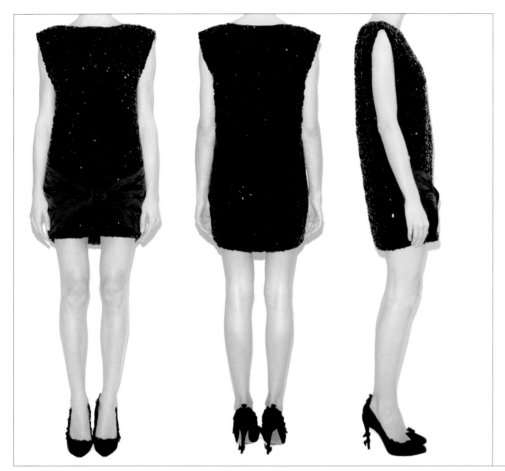

DESCRIPTION Sleeveless, all-over-beaded mini-dress with oversized bow detail in duchesse satin.

SWAROVSKI ELEMENTS
Hundreds of Galactic and Cosmic Sew-on Stones in various sizes, in color Jet.

SIZE US 6; UK 10; France 38; Italy 40; Germany 36; Japan 9

ESTIMATE see page 132

SHOES Alexis Mabille, not included

04 AZZARO

DESCRIPTION Strapless mini-dress in wool crepe with starburst embroidery and pleated trim.

SWAROVSKI ELEMENTS
Approximately 1,500 Chaton and Roses Montées elements in various sizes, in colors Jet, Jet Hematite, Black Diamond, and Crystal Silver Shade.

SIZE US 4; UK 8; France 36; Italy 38; Germany 34; Japan 7

ESTIMATE see page 132

SHOES Pierre Hardy, not included

DESCRIPTION Handmade white resin figurine wearing a beaded black net dress, inside a Victorian-style glass dome, with a floor of crystal-embellished paper.

SWAROVSKI ELEMENTS
Dozens of 2 and 3 mm (⅟₁₆ and ⅛ in.) Beads on figurine; Crystal-it motifs on the floor of the base, all in color Jet.

SIZE Height of dome: 80 cm/31½ in.; height of figurine: 31 cm/12¼ in.; area of base: 30 x 42 cm/11¾ x 16½ in.

ESTIMATE see page 132

CATHERINE MALANDRINO **06**

DESCRIPTION Cap-sleeved boat-neck shift dress in cashmere knit over metal rings, with a beige silk slip.

SWAROVSKI ELEMENTS
Approximately 800 Sew-on Stones in Rivoli, XILION, Galactic, Square, Rectangle, and Triangle shapes and cuts, in colors Crystal, Crystal Tabac, Sage, Olivine, Black Diamond, and Jet.

SIZE US 4; UK 8; France 36; Italy 38; Germany 34; Japan 7

ESTIMATE see page 132

SHOES Catherine Malandrino, not included

07 DIANE VON FURSTENBERG

DESCRIPTION Sundial-pleated wrap dress in a cotton-polyester blend, with silk organza and crystal picot-edged sleeves, a double-faced satin ribbon belt, and a ruffled hem.

SWAROVSKI ELEMENTS
The sleeves are fully covered with Chaton Bandings in colors Jet, Jet Hematite, and Crystal. On the belt, about 400 small XILION Beads, Navette, Drop, and Square Sew-on Stones; and Cosmic Rings, Triangles, and Square Rings, all in colors Crystal Satin and Jet.

SIZE US 4; UK 8; France 36; Italy 38; Germany 34; Japan 7

ESTIMATE see page 132

SHOES Pierre Hardy, not included

08 DONNA KARAN NEW YORK

DESCRIPTION Floor-length open-shoulder viscose jersey gown.

SWAROVSKI ELEMENTS
2,600 Avant-Garde, Galactic Vertical, and Horizontal Pendants, and Galactic Sew-on Stones in colors Crystal, Crystal Silver Shade, Jet, and Black Diamond.

SIZE US 4; UK 8; France 36; Italy 38; Germany 34; Japan 7

ESTIMATE see page 132

SHOES Donna Karan New York, not included

DESCRIPTION Patent nappa sheepskin apron dress with a bow-detailed collar and crystal-embellished front and back panels.

SWAROVSKI ELEMENTS
On panels and collar, dozens of Crystal Rivets in color Jet, as well as Crystal Pearls in tones of brown and black and in various sizes. On the sides, accents of Crystal Fabric in color Jet Hematite.

SIZE US 6; UK 10; France 38; Italy 40; Germany 36; Japan 9

ESTIMATE see page 132

SHOES Marios Schwab, not included

DESCRIPTION Duchesse satin and silk chiffon dress with layers of Crystal Aerial Mesh, an exposed zipper, and a corresponding headpiece.

SWAROVSKI ELEMENTS
Ten meters of Crystal Aerial Mesh with gold-cased crystals in color Jet, 38 Coral Pendants in color Crystal Red Magma; and Channel Web Sheets using gold-cased crystals in color Crystal Golden Shadow.

SIZE US 6; UK 10; France 38; Italy 40; Germany 36; Japan 9

ESTIMATE see page 132

SHOES Gaspard Yurkievich, not included

11 GIANFRANCO FERRÉ

DESCRIPTION Strapless, pleated mini-dress in silk gazar with an embellished, asymmetrical bow, duchesse satin sash, and silk velvet trim.

SWAROVSKI ELEMENTS
Various shapes of Sew-on Stones, Fancy Stones, and Beads in colors Jet, Jet Hematite, Jet Nut, Black Diamond, Crystal Tabac, Crystal Dorado, Crystal Silver Shade, and Crystal Copper.

SIZE US 6; UK 10; France 38; Italy 40; Germany 36; Japan 9

ESTIMATE see page 132

SHOES Christopher Kane, not included

12 GIORGIO ARMANI PRIVÉ

DESCRIPTION Draped, strapless net gown with an asymmetrical hem and a beaded flower at the waist.

SWAROVSKI ELEMENTS
Fishnet Banding with Jet-colored crystals all over the dress and embellished with Armani-designed Diamond Leaf Sew-on Stones. XILION Lochrose Sew-on Stones on flower detail, all in color Jet.

SIZE US 6; UK 10; France 38; Italy 40; Germany 36; Japan 9

ESTIMATE see page 132

SHOES Pierre Hardy, not included

DESCRIPTION Viscose and elastane beaded mini-dress with geometric cut-outs.

SWAROVSKI ELEMENTS
2,016 Square, Cosmic, and Triangle Sew-on Stones, in various sizes, in color Jet.

SIZE US 6; UK 10; France 38; Italy 40; Germany 36; Japan 9

ESTIMATE see page 132

SHOES Givenchy by Riccardo Tisci, not included

JEAN PAUL GAULTIER **14**

DESCRIPTION Silk taffeta cocktail dress with pleated hip pockets and organza hem inserts, featuring beaded front and back criss-cross straps that buckle in back.

SWAROVSKI ELEMENTS
Hundreds of large Rivoli Sew-on Stones and Crystal Buttons, as well as small sized Beads, all in color Jet.

SIZE US 4; UK 8; France 36; Italy 38; Germany 34; Japan 7

ESTIMATE see page 132

SHOES Jean Paul Gaultier, not included

15 LANVIN BY ALBER ELBAZ

DESCRIPTION Sleeveless trapeze dress with cut-through seams at the shoulders, embroidered silk tulle on the front, and a long satin sash.

SWAROVSKI ELEMENTS
Dozens of Sew-on Stones in XILION, Square Lochrose, and Navette cuts, in colors Crystal and Crystal Satin.

SIZE US 4; UK 8; France 36; Italy 38; Germany 34; Japan 7

ESTIMATE see page 132

SHOES Lanvin by Alber Elbaz, not included

16 MARIOS SCHWAB

DESCRIPTION Stretch grosgrain and powermesh sleeveless shift with a mesh insert and a horsehair-lined, molded bustle on the back.

SWAROVSKI ELEMENTS
Approximately 250 Cosmic, Galactic, and Diamond Leaf Sew-on Stones in colors Crystal and Crystal Silver Shade, in various sizes.

SIZE US 4; UK 8; France 36; Italy 38; Germany 34; Japan 7

ESTIMATE see page 132

SHOES Pierre Hardy, not included

DESCRIPTION Wool and silk cap-sleeved, hourglass shift entirely covered with crystals.

SWAROVSKI ELEMENTS
Thousands of XILION Transfers of various sizes in colors Jet, Jet Hematite, Black Diamond, Crystal, and Crystal Silver Shade.

SIZE US 6; UK 10; France 38; Italy 40; Germany 36; Japan 9

ESTIMATE see page 132

SHOES Pierre Hardy, not included

DESCRIPTION Sleeveless, Crystal Fabric, silk and Lurex® shift with an asymmetrical shoulder line on the back.

SWAROVSKI ELEMENTS
Layers of Crystal Fabric and three large Fancy Stones in color Jet Hematite.

SIZE US 6; UK 10; France 38; Italy 40; Germany 36; Japan 9

ESTIMATE see page 132

SHOES Missoni, not included

19 SONIA RYKIEL

DESCRIPTION Extra-fine merino wool halter dress with a ruffled hem and a cotton knitted bolero.

SWAROVSKI ELEMENTS
XILION Transfers in color Crystal spell out *Tête d'Affiche*, across the front of the dress.

SIZE US 4; UK 8; France 36; Italy 38; Germany 34; Japan 7

ESTIMATE see page 132

SHOES Sonia Rykiel, not included

20 THAKOON

DESCRIPTION Black sleeveless crepe de chine shift with crystal-embellished elastic panels and an exposed double-zipper.

SWAROVSKI ELEMENTS
Transfers consisting of a mix of Creation Stones in various shapes, all in color Jet.

SIZE US 4; UK 8; France 36; Italy 38; Germany 34; Japan 7

ESTIMATE see page 132

SHOES Pierre Hardy, not included

DESCRIPTION Boat-necked, long-sleeved mini-shift in silk gazar with a wire and Crystal Yarn web running along the shoulders and sleeves.

SWAROVSKI ELEMENTS
Yards of Crystal Yarn and hundreds of Beads and Briolette Pendants in colors Jet and Black Diamond woven into the web.

SIZE US 4; UK 8; France 36; Italy 38; Germany 34; Japan 7

ESTIMATE see page 132

SHOES Valentino, not included

DESCRIPTION Ruched, silver-backed black duchesse satin dress worn with separate crystal-embellished tie-on cape and peplum made out of duchesse satin.

SWAROVSKI ELEMENTS
Accents of Crystal Mesh in colors Crystal Silver Shade, Crystal Copper, Light Colorado Topaz, and Crystal Golden Shadow.

SIZE US 6; UK 10; France 38; Italy 40; Germany 36; Japan 9

ESTIMATE see page 132

SHOES Pierre Hardy, not included

GUIDE FOR PROSPECTIVE BUYERS

BUYING AT AUCTION

The following pages are designed to offer you information on how to buy at this charity auction at Phillips de Pury & Company. Our staff will be happy to assist you.

PRIOR TO AUCTION

Pre-Sale Estimates

Pre-sale estimates are intended as a guide for prospective buyers. Any bid within the high and low estimate range should, in our opinion, offer a chance of success. However, many lots achieve prices below or above the pre-sale estimates.
For further information on **ESTIMATES for each lot, please contact the specialist department or visit www.swarovski-elements.com/black**. It is advisable to contact us closer to the time of the auction as estimates can be subject to revision. Pre-sale estimates do not include any applicable taxes.

Pre-Sale Estimates in Pounds Sterling and Euros

Although the sale is conducted in US dollars, the pre-sale estimates may also be indicated in pounds sterling and/or euros. Since the exchange rate is that at the time of catalogue production and not at the date of auction, you should treat estimates in pounds sterling or euros as a guide only.

Condition of Lots

All prospective buyers are encouraged to inspect the lots at the pre-sale exhibitions (dates and hours to be announced online at www.swarovski-elements.com/black). Phillips de Pury & Company and Swarovski accept no liability for the condition of the lots.

Reserve

All lots in this catalogue are offered subject to a reserve. A reserve is the confidential value established between Swarovski and Phillips de Pury & Company and below which a lot may not be sold. The reserve for each lot is generally set at a percentage of the low estimate and will not exceed the low pre-sale estimate.

BIDDING IN THE SALE

Bidding at Auction

Bids may be executed during the auction in person by paddle or by telephone or prior to the sale in writing by absentee bid.

Bidding in Person

To bid in person, you will need to register for and collect a paddle before the auction begins. Proof of identity in the form of government issued identification will be required, as will an original signature. We may also require that you furnish us with a bank reference. New clients are encouraged to register at least 48 hours in advance of a sale to allow sufficient time for us to process your information. All lots sold will be invoiced to the name to which the paddle has been registered and invoices cannot be transferred to other names and addresses. Please do not misplace your paddle. In the event you lose it, inform a Phillips de Pury & Company staff member immediately. At the end of the auction, please return your paddle to the registration desk.

Bidding by Telephone

If you cannot attend the auction, you may bid live on the telephone with one of our multi-lingual staff members. This service must be arranged at least 24 hours in advance of the sale. Telephone bids may be recorded. By bidding on the telephone, you consent to the recording of your conversation. We suggest that you leave a maximum bid, excluding any applicable taxes, which we can execute on your behalf in the event we are unable to reach you by telephone.

Absentee Bids

If you are unable to attend the auction and cannot participate by telephone, Phillips de Pury & Company will be happy to execute written bids on your behalf. An "Absentee Bid Form" is available from Phillips de Pury & Company. This service is free and confidential. Bids must be placed in the currency of the sale. Our staff will attempt to execute an absentee bid at the lowest possible price taking into account the reserve and other bidders. Always indicate a maximum bid, excluding any applicable taxes. Unlimited bids will not be accepted. Any absentee bid must be received at least 24 hours in advance of the sale. In the event of identical bids, the earliest bid received will take precedence.

Bidding Increments

Bidding generally opens below the low estimate and advances in increments of up to 10%, subject to the auctioneer's discretion. Absentee bids that do not conform to the increments set below may be lowered to the next bidding increment.

$50 to $1,000	by $50s
$1,000 to $2,000	by $100s
$2,000 to $3,000	by $200s
$3,000 to $5,000	by $200s, 500, 800
	(i.e. $4,200, 4,500, 4,800)
$5,000 to $10,000	by $500s
$10,000 to $20,000	by $1,000s
$20,000 to $30,000	by $2,000s
$30,000 to $50,000	by $2,000s, 5,000, 8,000
$50,000 to $100,000	by $5,000s
$100,000 to $200,000	by $10,000s
above $200,000	auctioneer's discretion

The auctioneer may vary the increments during the course of the auction at his or her own discretion.

THE AUCTION

Consecutive and Responsive Bidding
The auctioneer may open the bidding on any lot by placing a bid on behalf of the seller. The auctioneer may further bid on behalf of the seller up to the amount of the reserve by placing consecutive bids or bids in response to other bidders. If a lot is not sold, the auctioneer will announce that it has been 'passed', 'withdrawn', 'returned to owner' or 'bought-in'.

Successful Bids
At this charity auction, the final bid price, or hammer price, shall be the purchase price. Phillips de Pury & Company will not levy any buyer's premium or other commission on the hammer price. However, sales tax, use tax, excise tax and other taxes are payable on the purchase price as required by applicable law.

AFTER THE AUCTION

Payment
Buyers are required to pay for purchases immediately following the auction unless other arrangements are agreed with Swarovski in writing in advance of the sale. Payments must be made in US dollars check drawn on a US bank or wire transfer, made payable to Swarovski. 100% of the proceeds are donated by Swarovski in equal part to The American Cancer Society and to la Ligue nationale contre le cancer, France.

Collection
Swarovski requires proof of identity on collection of a lot. A lot will be released to the buyer or the buyer's authorized representative when Swarovski has received full and cleared payment of the purchase price plus all applicable taxes. All purchased items should be collected within the 30 days following the sale, from Swarovski.

Loss or Damage
Buyers are advised that Phillips de Pury & Company and Swarovski accept no liability for loss or damage to lots and that they should arrange for their own insurance for the purchased lots.

Transport and Shipping
Buyers are advised that the organization and payment of shipping and transport of the purchased lots are the sole responsibility of the buyer.

Export and Import Licenses
Before bidding for any property, prospective bidders are advised to make independent inquiries as to whether a license is required to export the property from the United States or to import it into another country. It is the buyer's sole responsibility to comply with all import and export laws and to obtain any necessary licenses or permits. The denial of any required license or permit or any delay in obtaining such documentation will not justify the cancellation of the sale or any delay in making full payment for the lot.

Endangered Species
Items made of or incorporating plant or animal material, such as coral, crocodile, ivory, whalebone, rhinoceros horn or tortoiseshell, irrespective of age, percentage or value, may require a license or certificate prior to exportation and additional licenses or certificates upon importation to any foreign country. Please note that the ability to obtain an export license or certificate does not ensure the ability to obtain an import license or certificate in another country, and vice versa. We suggest that prospective bidders check with their own government regarding wildlife import requirements prior to placing a bid. It is the buyer's sole responsibility to obtain any necessary export or import licenses or certificates as well as any other required documentation. The denial of any required license or certificate or any delay in obtaining such documentation will not justify the cancellation of the sale or any delay in making full payment for the lot.

MISCELLANEOUS LIMITATION OF LIABILITY
Phillips de Pury & Company and Swarovski (i) are not liable for any errors or omissions, whether orally or in writing, in information provided to prospective buyers by Phillips de Pury & Company, Swarovski or any affiliated companies (ii) do not accept responsibility to any bidder in respect of acts of omissions, whether negligent or otherwise, by Phillips de Pury & Company, Swarovski or any affiliated companies in connection with the conduct of the auction or for any other matter relating to the sale of any lot.

LAW AND JURISDICTION
The rights and obligations of the parties with respect to this charity auction, the conduct of the auction and any matters related to any of the foregoing shall be governed by and interpreted in accordance with laws of the State of New York, excluding its conflicts of law rules.

PHILLIPS
de PURY & COMPANY

SWAROVSKI ELEMENTS

SWAROVSKI ELEMENTS is the product brand for the world's finest loose cut crystals manufactured by Swarovski. Available in myriad colors, effects, shapes, and sizes, these elements provide a palette of inspiration for designers in the worlds of fashion, jewelry, accessories, and interior design. The "MADE WITH SWAROVSKI ELEMENTS" tag serves as a guarantee of quality, authenticity, and integrity.

Since 1895, Swarovski has been the industry's unparalleled leader in creativity with crystals, and today, with a presence in over 120 countries, the company is proud to be in partnership with practitioners in all fields of design.

www.swarovski-elements.com

PHILLIPS
de PURY & COMPANY

Founded in London in 1796, Phillips de Pury & Company is unique among the three leading international auction houses for its focus on contemporary art and culture. The house that once enjoyed the patronage of such clients as Marie Antoinette, Beau Brummel, and Napoleon Bonaparte has become a recognized tastemaker in the contemporary field. With architecturally acclaimed galleries in London and New York, auction catalogues containing daring covers and content, and an exclusive partnership with London's Saatchi Gallery, Phillips de Pury & Company is courting a new generation of art lovers.

Headquartered in New York and London, with offices throughout the world, Phillips de Pury & Company holds sales in a limited number of categories: Contemporary Art, Design, Photographs, Editions, and Jewelry. This allows the company to better target clients with personalized service, making a maximum impact with its expertise and continuing to set records in these collecting fields.

www.phillipsdepury.com

THE OFFICIAL SPONSOR OF BIRTHDAYS.

The American Cancer Society combines an unyielding passion with nearly a century of experience to save lives and end suffering from cancer. As a global grassroots force of more than three million volunteers, and more than 3,400 local offices nationwide, it saves lives by helping people stay well by preventing cancer or detecting it early; helps people get well by supporting people during and after a cancer diagnosis; finds cures through investment in groundbreaking discovery; and fights back by rallying legislators to pass laws to combat cancer and inspiring communities worldwide to join the fight.

As the United States' largest non-governmental investor in cancer research, contributing about $3.4 billion to date, the American Cancer Society funds research that helps us understand cancer's causes and cures. As a result, more than 11 million people who have survived cancer, and countless others who have avoided it, will be celebrating birthdays this year.

www.cancer.org

Established in Paris in 1918, la Ligue nationale contre le cancer is a non-profit association with 740,000 members and countless volunteers across France. A federation of 103 regional committees, it is France's first independent provider of financial support for cancer research. Today, la Ligue supports innovative, world-class research into all aspects of the disease, and acts to reduce its incidence through public awareness campaigns, training for health professionals, and early detection and diagnosis efforts.

Through its local offices, la Ligue is a source of practical, emotional, and financial support to cancer patients, survivors, and their families. With its patient-centered approach and multiple fronts of action, la Ligue's aim is quite simply to stop the progression of this devastating disease.

www.ligue-cancer.net

PAGE 62 - 63
PHOTOGRAPHY Mark Pillai

PAGE 64 - 65
PHOTOGRAPHY Mark Pillai

PAGE 66 - 67
PHOTOGRAPHY Mark Pillai

PAGE 68 - 69 PHOTOGRAPHY Mark Pillai
SHOES Pierre Hardy

PAGE 70 - 71 PHOTOGRAPHY Mark Pillai
SHOES Donna Karan New York

PAGE 72 - 73
PHOTOGRAPHY Scheltens & Abbenes

PAGE 74 - 75
PHOTOGRAPHY Mark Pillai

PAGE 76 - 77
PHOTOGRAPHY Mark Pillai

PAGE 78 - 79
PHOTOGRAPHY Mark Pillai

PAGE 80 - 81
PHOTOGRAPHY Scheltens & Abbenes

PAGE 82 - 83
PHOTOGRAPHY Mark Pillai

PAGE 84 - 85 PHOTOGRAPHY Mark Pillai
SHOES Christopher Kane

PAGE 86 - 87
PHOTOGRAPHY Mark Pillai

PAGE 88 - 89
PHOTOGRAPHY Scheltens & Abbenes

PAGE 90 - 91 PHOTOGRAPHY Mark Pillai
SHOES Pierre Hardy

PAGE 92 - 93
PHOTOGRAPHY Mark Pillai

PAGE 94 - 95
PHOTOGRAPHY Scheltens & Abbenes

PAGE 96 - 97 PHOTOGRAPHY Mark Pillai
SHOES Donna Karan New York

PAGE 98 - 99
PHOTOGRAPHY Mark Pillai

PAGE 100 - 101
PHOTOGRAPHY Mark Pillai

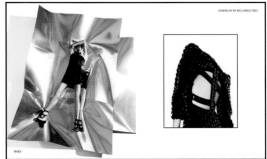

PAGE 102 - 103 PHOTOGRAPHY Mark Pillai
SHOES Marios Schwab

PAGE 104 - 105
PHOTOGRAPHY Mark Pillai

PAGE 106 - 107
PHOTOGRAPHY Scheltens & Abbenes

PAGE 108 - 109
PHOTOGRAPHY Mark Pillai

PAGE 110 - 111
PHOTOGRAPHY Mark Pillai

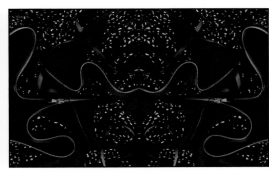

PAGE 112 - 113
PHOTOGRAPHY Scheltens & Abbenes

PAGE 114 - 115
PHOTOGRAPHY Mark Pillai

PAGE 116 - 117 PHOTOGRAPHY Mark Pillai
SHOES Valentino

PAGE 118 - 119 PHOTOGRAPHY Mark Pillai
SHOES Pierre Hardy

FASHION PHOTOGRAPHY
PHOTOGRAPHER Mark Pillai @ Artlist
STYLIST Hector Castro
FASHION ASSISTANT Gretchen Owen
HAIR Tomohiro @ MAO
MAKEUP Alice Ghendrih @ Artlist
MANICURIST Elsa Durrens @ Artlist
SET DESIGNER Louis Benzoni @ Artlist
SET DESIGN ASSISTANT François Valenza
PHOTO ASSISTANTS Gregory Gex & Sascha Heintze
RETOUCHER Marjorie Lopez @ PX1 Berlin
DIGITAL ASSISTANT Sam Hendel @ DDC
STUDIO Studio Rouchon, Paris
LOCATION Domaine National de Saint-Cloud, Ile-de-France
PRODUCTION Julie Berton @ Artlist and Bruno Semeraro
DRIVER Joachim @ Milou
MODELS Alexandra Tretter @ Elite Model Management, Tanya Ilieva @ Silent Models, Claire Galtier @ Sport Models

STILL LIFE PHOTOGRAPHY
PHOTOGRAPHER Maurice Scheltens & Liesbeth Abbenes @ Art Department Europe
STYLIST Hector Castro
FASHION ASSISTANT Gretchen Owen
SET DESIGNER Liesbeth Abbenes
RETOUCHER Jan Hibma
DIGITAL OPERATOR Nicolas Receveur @ Studio Zéro
CONSTRUCTION Matthieu Botrel
CONSTRUCTION ASSISTANT Gaël Leroux
LIGHTING EQUIPMENT Pierre Olivier @ Studio Zéro
STUDIO Studio Zéro, Paris
PRODUCTION Therese Lundström

SPECIAL THANKS
Antony Miles, Julie Berton @ Artlist, Ingrid Janowski @ Art Department Europe, Bruno Semeraro, James Titterton, Peter Fenn, Jesper Richardy

SWAROVSKI'S *guarantee* OF CRYSTAL *perfection*

MADE WITH

SWAROVSKI
ELEMENTS